Dolls now and long ago

Carole Beaty

This book tells you about the dolls children have played with over the years. The book starts with dolls you see in the shops now and it then moves back into history.

You do not have to read this book from beginning to end. You can just turn to the pages that interest you.

Contents

Dolls nowadays

Many children like to play with dolls. You can go to many different sorts of shops to buy dolls.

⬆ You can go with your family to a big toy shop to buy your dolls.

Nowadays, dolls are made in factories.
Then they are sent to the shops.

There are lots of different dolls to choose from.

Most dolls you see in the shops are made of plastic.

Long ago dolls were made of different materials
like wax and wood. This book tells you which
materials were used.

1990s

3

Dolls in World War Two

In the Second World War there was a clever doll maker. She was called Norah Wellings. The dolls she made were soft and cuddly.

⬧ All these dolls are in uniform.

Norah Wellings made her dolls out of felt and velvet, which made them soft and cuddly. She designed all the dolls herself. Then they were made in large factories.

The heads of the dolls were moulded on a special machine that pushed out the noses and cheeks.

⬆ You can see Norah Wellings' label on the bottom of a doll's foot.

⬆ Some people made dolls at home to send to their friends and family.

Dolls and dolls' houses

Many small dolls are made to fit into dolls' houses. Dolls' houses were very popular long ago.

If you go to Windsor Castle you can see Queen Mary's dolls' house. It was a present for Queen Mary.

⬆ Queen Mary's dolls' house was designed by Sir Edwin Lutyens.

All the things inside work. There are electric lights that can go off and on. Hot and cold water comes out of the taps. There are even tiny keys to lock the doors.

1920s

7

Dolls in World War One

In the First World War a lot of people made their own dolls.

⬆ This doll could dance.

Some of the soldiers who were fighting in the war made dolls out of wood. They found the wood on the battlefield. The soldiers made the dolls when they were waiting for a battle to begin.

Some of the dolls were made in factories.
They were dressed in uniform.

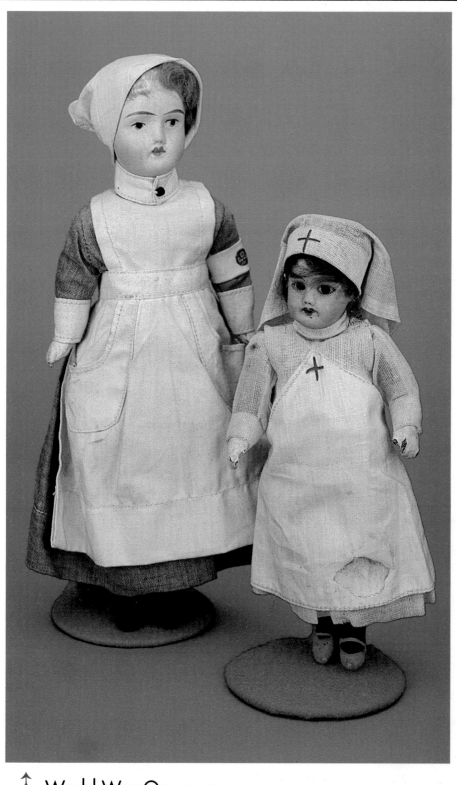

⬆ World War One nurses.

Celluloid dolls

Long ago, some dolls were made from celluloid. Celluloid is very strong.

If you dropped these dolls they did not break. Many dolls made with other materials could break.

◄◄ This celluloid doll has moulded hair.

Many of the celluloid dolls had faces that were made in a metal mould. Some of the dolls had a celluloid head which was stuck onto the leather body.

Sometimes the hair was made of mohair wool and the eyes were made of glass.

⬆ This celluloid doll has a leather body.

Wax dolls

Lots of dolls in Victorian times were made out of wax.
Wax is the material that candles are made of. When wax is hot it becomes soft and you can mould it.

This doll is over a hundred years old.

In the olden days doll makers used beeswax to make wax dolls. They mixed colours into the wax to make it look like skin.

The doll usually had a wax head, arms and legs, but the body was made out of cloth or leather. The hair was usually pushed into the soft wax.

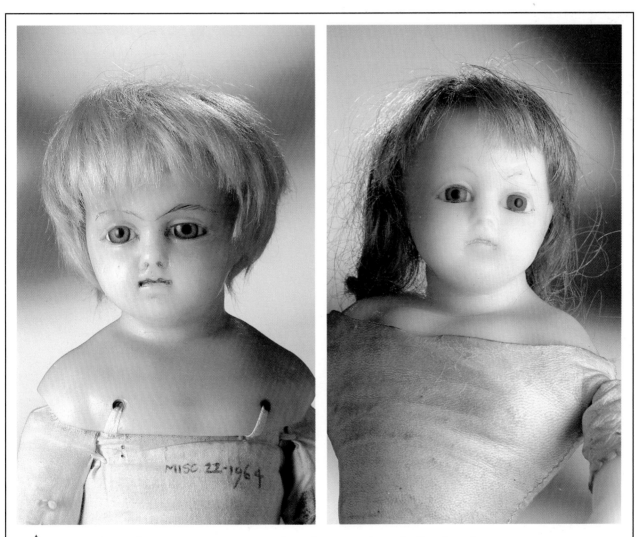

⬆ Wax heads were sewn or glued onto the dolls' bodies.

Gutta-percha dolls

Some dolls long ago were made of gutta-percha. Gutta-percha is a kind of rubber.

Gutta-percha trees grow in Malaysia. If you make a cut in a gutta-percha tree, some white liquid comes out. If you make the liquid hot it becomes stretchy and it can be made into shapes.

Doll-makers used to make the head and the arms of their dolls from gutta-percha. The doll maker usually painted the face on.

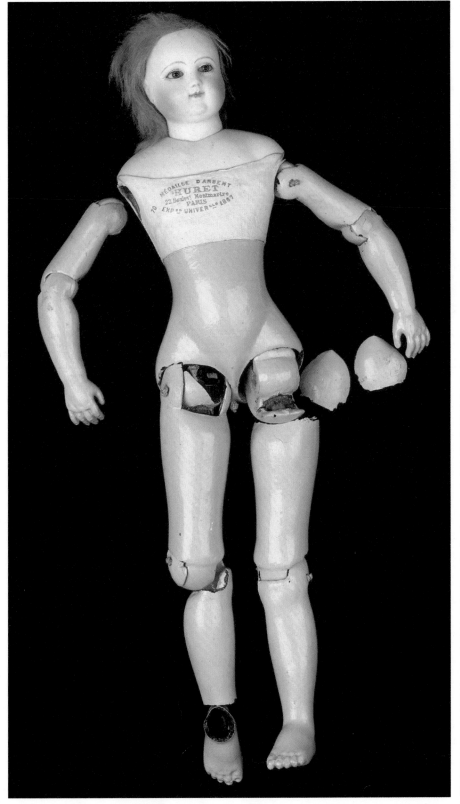

↞ This doll was made in France. She is over a hundred years old.

Paper dolls and theatres

Dolls and dolls' theatres can be made out of paper. Long ago children cut out dolls to play with.

◀◀ The dolls are pushed and pulled by using a piece of wire.

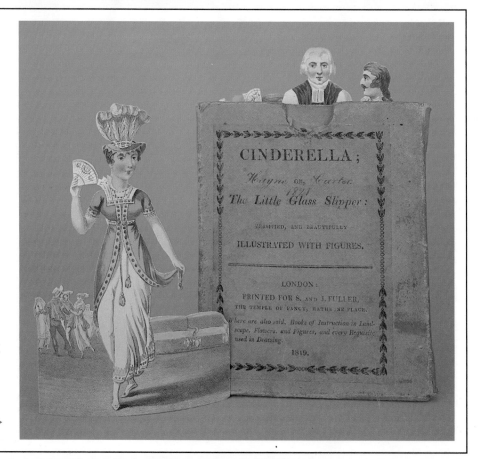

Children could cut out people from this book about Cinderella. ➤

You can still buy cut out dolls and theatres at the Pollocks Toy Museum in London.

When you visit the museum the shopkeeper shows you lots of different dolls and theatres. The shopkeeper also shows you how the dolls move.

Parian ware dolls

Parian ware dolls were popular in Victorian times. They looked like real people but they could easily break if you dropped them.

Parian ware is like china, which is the material cups and mugs are made of.

In 1851 a Great Exhibition was held in a building called the Crystal Palace. The new Parian ware dolls were on display.

In this building called the Crystal Palace, many people were excited to see the new Parian ware dolls.

↟ These dolls have glass eyes and painted eyelashes.

Homemade dolls

Long ago many children had no money to buy dolls, so they made their own dolls. They used things they could find in their own homes.

↑ A doll made out of an old boot.

In Victorian times some people were very poor so they could not buy dolls made out of china or wax.

They made their own dolls out of things they found at home. They used old wooden spoons and mops, even old bones or a boot.

We can still make dolls out of round clothes pegs. These are called "dolly pegs".

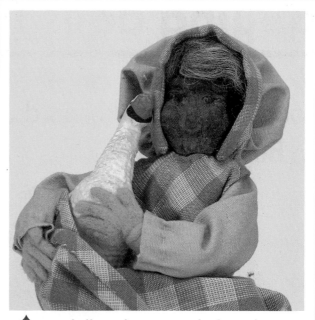

⬆ A doll with an apple head.

⬆ Dolls made out of an old spoon and a big bone.

1830

Buying dolls long ago

Long ago children could go to a fair
to buy toys.

Children went to a fair with their family to find their best doll.
They really liked the St Bartholomew's fairs, which were held
every year.

Glossary of words used in this book

Celluloid   Celluloid is a thin plastic.

Crystal Palace   Crystal Palace was a huge building that was built in 1851.
It was made of glass and iron.

Electric lights   Electric lights are lamps that are worked by electricity.

Felt   Felt is a thick cloth. It is made of wool.

First World War   The First World War was a war in which many countries took part.
It was fought mainly in Europe. It lasted from 1914 to 1918 and
many thousands of people were killed in this war.

Malaysia   Malaysia is a country very far away from Britain, in East Asia.
The weather is very hot and sticky in Malaysia.

Mohair wool   Mohair wool is a thick, fluffy material. The wool comes from a goat
called the Angora goat.

Mould   A mould is a hollow shape which is filled with material.
The mould forms the material into a shape.

Moulded   Moulded material has been put in a mould to make it into
a particular shape.

Parian ware   Parian ware is a fine material. It is like delicate pottery or china.
It can break easily.

Plastic   Plastic is a strong, light material. Plastic toys and dolls can be made in
many different shapes.

Queen Mary   Queen Mary was born in 1867 and died in 1953.
She was married to King George the Fifth.

St Bartholomew's fair   St Bartholomew's fair was an open-air market where you could
shop outside. You could buy toys and sweets at this fair.

Second World War   The Second World War was a war in which many countries took part.
It lasted from 1939 to 1945 and many thousands of people were
killed in the fighting.

Velvet   Velvet is a soft material. It has one furry side and one smooth side.

Victorian   Victorian things come from the time when Queen Victoria was Queen
of this country. This was from 1837 to 1901.

Wax   Wax is a yellow or white material made by bees. It can be made soft.
When it is soft it can be moulded.

Index

a b c d e f g h i j k l m n o p q r s t u v w x y z
A B C D E F G H I J K L M N O P Q R S T U V W X Y Z